4/49

AN ADELPHI BY-WAY

George Court, leading from the Strand into the Adelphi; part of it was the old-time
Of Alley, one of those linked by-ways of the York Buildings the names of which
together represented the full name of George Villiers, Duke of Buckingham.

IN LONDON'S BY-WAYS

Text by Walter Jerrold

Pictures by E. W. Haslehust, R.B.A.

BLACKIE & SON LIMITED
LONDON AND GLASGOW

BLACKIE & SON LIMITED
66 Chandos Place, London
17 Stanhope Street, Glasgow

BLACKIE & SON (INDIA) LIMITED
103/5 Fort Street, Bombay

BLACKIE & SON (CANADA) LIMITED
Toronto

BEAUTIFUL ENGLAND

Chester.

Windsor Castle.

Rambles in Greater London.

In London's By-ways.

The Thames.

The Peak District.

The Cornish Riviera.

Oxford.

Canterbury.

Shakespeare-land.

Exeter.

Dickens-land.

Through London's Highways.

The Heart of London.

Bath and Wells.

Winchester.

Dartmoor.

Cambridge.

York.

The English Lakes.

BEAUTIFUL SCOTLAND

Loch Lomond, Loch Katrine and the Trossachs.

The Scott Country.

Edinburgh.

The Shores of Fife.

BEAUTIFUL IRELAND

Ulster.

Munster.

Printed in Great Britain by Blackie & Son, Ltd., Glasgow

LIST OF ILLUSTRATIONS

"VENICE IN LONDON", PADDINGTON

Where the Grand Junction Canal and the Regent's Canal come together; much the same view, which he named "Venice in London", that Robert Browning had from the windows of 19 Warwick Crescent, his home for quarter of a century.

IN LONDON'S BY-WAYS

I

"Gem of all joy, jasper of jocundity,
　Most mighty carbuncle of virtue and valour,
Strong Troy in vigour and in strenuity,
　Of royal cities rose and geraflour;
Empress of townès, exalt in honour,
　In beauty bearing the throne imperial,
Sweet Paradise, precelling in pleasure:
London." 　　　　　　　*—William Dunbar.*

The droll exaggeration of the ancient Scots poet's
tribute to London may sound even as nonsense in
the ears of many present-day Londoners. It must
be recalled, however, that it was inspired by the
London of some four centuries since—a London
characterized by the opulent splendour of the early

Tudors; a London so remote from that of to-day that but few outstanding stones of it, away from the Tower of London, the Temple Church, Westminster Abbey, and Lambeth Palace, could be found by the careful searcher of the great City's highways and by-ways. There are many people who would cordially echo the sentiment, though they might boggle at the phrasing, of the Scotsman's tribute.

London can, indeed, no longer be summed up as a "gem": it has long lacked such essential unity as would justify the figure; it is an agglomeration of cities, towns, and villages that are to-day comprised within its loosely linking name. The square mile of that central City which represented London to one who was in his prime when the fifteenth century passed has come to be multiplied a vast number of times; London has indeed ceased to have the unity of a City and has become as it were an urban confederation. For the vast majority of us it is sufficient to know its story in parts—to know something of the districts in which we have occasion, for one reason or another, to take a particular interest. It is, perhaps, better so; we are thus always getting fresh glimpses of an infinite variety, that age cannot wither nor custom stale, fresh knowledge of an inexhaustible past.

Alike along the highways and about an infinite

of by-ways are to be found great diversity of things to attract and hold the attention, to stimulate the imagination and awaken the interest. Yet great are the material changes that have taken place within the memory of people still living. The march of improvement which has more than once revolutionized conditions of road transport, has meant a tendency to the making of wider and straighter main thorough-fares: Fleet Street is ceasing to be the Fleet Street that Samuel Johnson knew; the Strand is another Strand than that in which Charles Lamb declared that he shed tears "from fulness of joy at so much life". Apart from outstanding public buildings, when road widenings become necessary little of ancientry is allowed to remain. The low timbered houses of early times have given way to loftier buildings of brick and stone; so that a highway "bit" such as that of the Tudor entrance to Staple Inn by Holborn Bars remains unique, a museum specimen, as it were, preserved on its original site. Now brick and stone are so rapidly giving way to still higher stone-faced iron buildings that in a generation or two even eighteenth-century brickwork will need seeking in the by-ways—indeed it is there already that its most notable examples must be sought. Although, generally speaking, it may be said that changes in the by-ways of the metropolis are more gradual than in the highways, yet within the past century whole "areas" have been cleared, replanned, and rebuilt. Among such are notably Trafalgar Square, the Kingsway-Aldwych area, the St. Giles' "Rookery". Such by-ways as the Bermudas and Porridge Island are lost in the history of Trafalgar Square; Holywell and Wych Streets have more recently passed into the merely traditional.

It is in the by-ways that many of the older, quainter, and more picturesque "bits", the homes and haunts of the famous and interesting personages of the past, must be sought. A few hundred yards from where the Regent's Canal passes under the Edgware Road, for instance, we may come to the point at which that canal and the Grand Junction Canal join —a point which Robert Browning happily summed up as Venice in London. And here as in the treating of most other aspects of London any method of presentation, other than the merely catalogical, must be arbitrarily selective and broadly indicative rather than in any sense exhaustive. The field for exploration is inexhaustibly large, and the ways of exploring it must be governed by the particular interests, historical or architectural, picturesque or personal of the individual explorer.

II

"Reader, in the course of my peregrinations about the great city, it is hard if I have not picked up matter which may serve to amuse thee."—*Charles Lamb.*

Although among certain persons there is a common tendency to regard a museum as a musty, fusty, dusty accumulation of odd things, it has really come to be something widely different from that idea of it persistently propounded by the traditional humorist. The museum has come to be a quickening centre of knowledge—a super-library, as it were, where *things* may be systematically read instead of words about them as in books; a focal point where time and space are brought into unity. In such focal points London is peculiarly rich. Just beyond the point where the western end of Pall Mall and the southern end of St. James's Street angle together by the picturesque Tudor gatehouse of St. James's Palace, is what may be regarded as the best of all places from which to start any exploration of the by-ways of London, and whether we wish to explore London's by-ways as they are to-day, or to search in the by-ways of the past, we shall find in the London Museum what is without doubt the most fascinating and stimulating of starting-places.

Here, in a magnificent mansion built in 1825, is housed a collection which brings to the eye, as far as may be, the story of London from prehistoric times to the latest coronation. The building is a particularly handsome quadrangular one occupying the south-western corner of the district of St. James's, its western side looking out over the Green Park and its southern side over St. James's Park—with a wonderful panoramic view from the upper windows, ranging from Whitehall by way of the Houses of Parliament, Westminster Abbey, and the campanile of Westminster Cathedral to Buckingham Palace and Hyde Park Corner. After being known as York House, this mansion was renamed Stafford House when bought from the Crown in 1841 by the Duke of Sutherland. It was again renamed Lancaster House after being purchased by Lord Leverhulme who presented it to the nation for the housing of the London Museum, which was established to commemorate the coronation of King George the Fifth in 1911. The £72,000 which was realized by the sale of the property in 1841 was devoted in the following year to the purchasing of Victoria Park, as a recreation ground for the people; so that with the two beautiful West End parks on which we look from the windows here we may associate that yet more beautiful Victoria Park—more extensive than these two together—

which was so happily preserved as a pleasaunce for the people of the East End.

Though I have said that this London Museum is the most appropriate place at which to linger before setting out on any systematic excursions into London's by-ways, it is not, of course, possible to attempt anything in the nature of a detailed examination of the wonderful miscellany of things that have here been brought together. Here, however, may be seen things —recovered by excavation of the ground, and from dredging in the muddy deposits of the Thames— which serve to illustrate not only the London that was before any stone of its existing oldest buildings was quarried, but even afford glimpses of that long past when the earliest beginnings of the settlement that was to grow into London consisted of but a few primitive dwellings built on piles driven into the shallower waters of the Thames. The river was then much wider—extending it is said from Wandsworth to Ealing—and it is from the gravel deposits of that ancient river bed that evidence has been recovered of the presence hereabouts of Palæolithic man. Flint, horn, and early bronze implements are to be seen that indicate and illustrate successive stages in that indefinite era known as the "prehistoric period".

The London Museum has, however, still more to show that is of deepest interest when we come to

the historic period when the City was in the stages
of its early and growing importance. Apart from the
fragment of London Stone encaged within the outer
wall of the church of St. Swithin in Cannon Street,
some scanty portions of the City's earliest circumval-
lation, and the bath unearthed in a Strand by-way,
we can see little evidence of the days when, in the
early centuries of our era, London was the centre of
a Roman colony. Here in the Museum, however,
apart from the many smaller relics that have been
dug up—wonderful examples of coins, pottery, &c.—
there is one thing that I find more moving than any
other. Stones and mortar have a permanency which
makes their age unimpressive when compared with
less enduring materials: the Roman occupation seems
at a dateless distance as represented by its remaining
fragments of London's Wall; it seems but recent
when we stand in the basement of Lancaster House
and look upon the wonderfully preserved remains of
a Roman galley, supposed to be a part of the fleet
of Carausius, sunk in the Thames about the close of
the third century. This was discovered near the
eastern end of Westminster Bridge when the foundations were being dug for the building of the London
County Hall. Near it in the Museum is a boat of
still earlier days, a large dug-out hollowed from an
oak trunk, that was recovered from the bed of the

CROOKED BILLET YARD, SHOREDITCH

One of the quaint and picturesque bits remaining—in greatly altered circumstances—to indicate
something of the character of the inn courtyards of the old coaching days.

river near Kew Bridge, where it must have lain preserved in the silt for perhaps a couple of thousand years.

These are things that to the imaginative bridge the centuries as it were by the shortest of short cuts, making us realize a past with which few direct links remain. There are countless others that will make us realize successive stages in the London of the historic past when wandering about it in the present. Among the most notable are the series of beautiful models of old London, a study of which is a pleasant preparation for wandering about the actual places as they have since come to be modified by the devastating hand of Time and his agents. Here, for instance, is London Bridge as it was when that gossiping Londoner Samuel Pepys walked on it, when it supported a street of houses before the Great Fire of 1666 demolished all. Here is Cheapside, seen as it was when that thoroughfare was a broad way of gabled houses; here is the old spired St. Paul's Cathedral as it was before being overwhelmed in the Great Fire. Here, too, is to be seen central London with that Cathedral in process of destruction by the fire, the illusion of flames being hinted at in ingenious fashion by the pulsating of miniature electric lights within the building. So valuable are these models as aids to the imagination that

it would be well if their number could be increased.
A similar model, in so far as it should prove recon-
structible, might well represent to the eye the old
walled Londinium of the Romans, and another might
help us to realize the old way from the City to Westminster Abbey when betwixt the Thames and the
Strand were mainly splendid mansions of the nobles.

There are innumerable other things that may be
usefully studied in the London Museum, things too
many and too varied for particularization. Mention
must be made, however, of the many capital photo-
graphs of houses associated with celebrated men and
women, and other notable buildings. Some day,
perhaps, the museum will be able to exhibit a com-
plete series of views of the houses that have been
thought worthy of being marked with commemorative
plaques; such a collection, arranged by districts,
accompanied by an alphabetical list of the persons
commemorated, would prove of real interest and help
to a large number of London lovers—residents and
visitors alike.

Though I have thus lightly indicated the London
Museum as an appropriate starting-point for any
intimate study of London, there are other collections
possessing notable relics of the great City's past. In
the Guildhall Museum much may be seen, includ-
ing fine specimens of Roman tessellated pavements

recovered from time to time during rebuilding opera-
tions in the City; for it has been said there are
probably but few Londoners who realize that, as
they walk about the central parts of their City, they
have, but a few feet beneath them, much that was
a part of the ancient Londinium. Much of old London in relic form may be found, too, in the great
collections of the British Museum and the Victoria
and Albert Museum.

Another museum, small and special, which serves
to illustrate the amenities of the lives of past
Londoners, though opened about ten years ago, seems
as yet known to comparatively few Londoners. This
is the Geffrye Museum, where, in a row of old
alms-houses built by Sir Thomas Geffrye, "alderman
and ironmonger", in 1703, is housed a wonderful
collection of examples of old furniture and domestic
craftsmanship of the period from the fifteenth to the
nineteenth century. From panelling to pewter ware,
from carved staircases to candle-snuffers, we may see
here what I once heard an old Whitechapel woman
describe neatly as the "domestic details" of bygone
London homes. The Museum will be found occupying those eighteenth-century alms-houses already
mentioned a little north of Shoreditch Church.
Between the railway bridges that cross the road near
this museum is a very quaint bit surviving in the

by-way of Crooked Billet Yard. This is a striking portion of the old-time courtyard inns.

III

"You are now
In London, that great sea, whose ebb and flow
At once is deaf and loud, and on the shore
Vomits its wrecks, and still howls on for more.
Yet in its depths what treasures!"

—*Percy Bysshe Shelley.*

The triumph of the motor as a means of road transport is causing a seemingly gradual but really rapid transformation of London. By-ways are being converted into highways by the inevitable processes of widening and straightening; whole street frontages are being entirely changed. In the course of a generation or two, as I lately heard it declared, London will probably be a very fine handsome city, but it will not be the London that people of middle age now living have known. What the more conservative among us do not perhaps sufficiently realize is that it has been thus for several centuries. Quite apart from the great rebuilding of central London consequent upon the devastating fire of two and a half centuries ago, the old has ever been giving way to the new. So much has this been the case that,

AMEN CORNER, PATERNOSTER ROW

Through a simple gateway near Amen Corner, at the western end of Paternoster Row
is Amen Court, one of the most pleasantly surprising of all the City's by-ways.

apart from churches, Inns of Court, and a few public edifices, any buildings of earlier date than the last years of the seventeenth century need to be searched for. The eighteenth century appears to have had a goodly wave of rebuilding energy, while both that century and the succeeding one saw a remarkable extension of residential London in all directions. Domestic architecture is that which, from a variety of causes, is the most rapidly variable, so that urban dwelling houses more than a couple of centuries old are rare indeed.

Glancing first at the by-ways in that central part of London anciently within the City gates—the positions of which remain indicated at Ludgate, Newgate, Moorgate, Aldersgate, Cripplegate, Bishopsgate, Aldgate, Billingsgate, and Dowgate—we shall find a network mostly of short narrow streets, lanes, alleys and courts dominated to-day by offices, warehouses and business premises of all sorts. In olden times when means of communication were slow and difficult there was a natural tendency for men engaged in the same trade to settle down about a common centre, and the result of this is sufficiently notable in the way in which special trades still predominate in certain of the City districts. North, east, and south of St. Paul's Cathedral will be found the warehouses and offices of those concerned in the

wholesale distribution of clothing materials and
millinery; publishing and allied businesses will be
found in large numbers to the north-west of the
Cathedral; shipping offices in and about Leadenhall
Street; insurance offices about Cornhill, and the fish
trade about Billingsgate and so on; the meat sales-
men in the neighbourhood of Smithfield and Farringdon
have but migrated a little from where their fore-
runners, the fleshers, congregated about Newgate
Street.

It has indeed been claimed for certain sagacious
persons that if dumped, blindfolded, in any of the
City's by-ways they could discover their whereabouts
by the pervading odour of the immediate district's
dominating trade. Billingsgate alone would be able
to afford that olfactory advertisement to some of us,
though it is certainly a very different atmosphere that
is inhaled but a little distance away about Mark
Lane, where we may breathe hints of all the spicy
fragrance of the East.

The settlement which grew to be London began,
in all probability, with a group of wattled huts on a
hill more or less surrounded by the marshy margin
of the Thames and certain small tributaries. On that
hill now stands St. Paul's Cathedral, a little to the
north of which, it is claimed, is the actual summit.
There, one of the shortest of the City's by-ways, link-

ing the eastern ends of Paternoster Row and Newgate Street, is Panyer Alley, almost wholly rebuilt,
wherein of old, says tradition, bakers' baskets were
sold. Let into a wall on the eastern side of it is to
be seen the figure of a naked child seated on a
pannier, and underneath the inscription—

> "When ye have sought
> the City Round
> Yet still this is
> The highest Ground
>
> August the 27
> 1688"

All about St. Paul's are by-ways the names of
which are linked with the history of the dominating
Cathedral: Paternoster Row itself, for long associated
with the wholesale book trade, is said to have been
originally the place where rosaries were sold, but I
like better the reason for its name given by an olden
writer who says "Paternoster Row was anciently so-
called on account of the number of stationers and
writers who lived there before the invention of the
noble art of printing; who wrote and sold the little
books most in use in those times of ignorance, as
alphabets with the Paternoster, the Ave Maria, the
Creed and Graces". Ave Maria Lane, Creed Lane,
Amen Court and Corner, Dean's Yard and Doctors'

Commons are other of the by-ways hereabouts
obviously owing their names to the contiguity of the
Cathedral.

Through a simple gateway near Amen Corner, at
the western end of Paternoster Row, is Amen Court,
one of the most surprising of all the City's by-ways.
Here are beautiful, secluded, old-fashioned houses
with greenery of lawns and shrubs—an oasis of calm
amid tumultuous streets. The handsome red-brick
Deanery will be found, shut in to dinginess, in the
brevity of Dean's Yard just south of the western end
of the Cathedral; the detached house having a
curiously old-world appearance amid crowding warehouses. Here we may go through to Doctors'
Commons—greatly changed since David Copperfield
passed hours of his romantic youth in the legal
office there of Messrs. Spenlow & Jorkins. Beyond
again, fronting on the highway of Queen Victoria
Street, is the Heralds' College, centre of romance
which is perhaps but a trifle more historical—that
which is blazoned in armorial bearings. Near by,
too, is the Church of St. Andrew by the Wardrobe
(rebuilt by Christopher Wren) and near it in the
tree-shaded Wardrobe Place are still some late
seventeenth-century houses. Near, too, is one of
the tiny churchyard fragments, shrub and ivy-grown,
which afford resting-spots for tired workers, and

WARDROBE PLACE, BLACKFRIARS

Near to Wren's church of St. Andrew by the Wardrobe, this quiet by-way affords a glimpse
of what a residential part of the City was like over two centuries ago.

memories of bygone churches. In this case the church was that of St. Ann's Blackfriars, which was not rebuilt after the Great Fire.

The small district here indicated is typical of the variety of interests that may be found all about the by-ways of Central London. Here are busy streets in which the work of to-day is being carried on by the army that each morning invades the City and each evening retires to far-scattered homes; and here and there in lesser by-ways and tiny courts are pleasant glimpses or reminders of the varying past. East of St. Paul's Cathedral in the by-ways lying between Cannon Street and Cheapside, again are to be found interesting old churches and scraps of the God's acre, once attached to churches that have disappeared—ivy-grown patches with maybe a few time-defaced gravestones, all that civic sentiment has permitted to remain of places where the citizens of old worshipped. Thanks to a growing regard for site values, and, it would seem, a diminishing regard for moral values, many more of the City churches are threatened with a demolition that will leave not a wrack behind.

Through this small tract was Watling Street, part of the important Roman highway diminished to the lane of a modern city. Hereabouts we may visit the place where of old stood "an ancient inn of

mullioned panes, and crazy beams and over-hanging
eaves"—that Mermaid Tavern the very name of
which brings to mind the wit and poetry and
splendid romance associated with the great men
of the Elizabethan age — all the wonder and delight
of which has been newly revived by Alfred Noyes
in his *Tales of the Mermaid Tavern*. From
Bread Street to Friday Street the old inn stretched;
in the first of these was John Milton born, while in
the second Geoffrey Chaucer once walked—one of the
few facts, trifling though it be, that we know of the
personal life of that poet. In Friday Street, too, met
that club at which William Paterson, "projector" and
founder of the Bank of England, schemed for the
union of England and Scotland. To divagate into
the by-ways of history attached to old-time buildings
of London would need a volume far larger than the
present, and that without ever getting beyond the
central square mile.

Crossing Cheapside and passing up Wood Street,
one of the many by-ways tangled beyond its northern
side, we presently arrive at the church where John
Milton is buried. This is St. Giles, Cripplegate,
where Frobisher the Elizabethan seaman, and Foxe,
author of the *Book of Martyrs*, are also buried,
and where Oliver Cromwell was married. As we go
along Wood Street we pass in the Wren-built church

of St. Alban's one of the oldest religious foundations
of London and the probable centre of the Saxon
City.   Milton's association with the district will be
found celebrated in Milton Street, believed to be
the old-time Grub Street of the hack writers.   Somewhat to the west is Little Britain, another centre
long associated with the bookselling business, leading through to the beautiful old church of St.
Bartholomew's, and so to the picturesque haven of
Charterhouse, and to the strangely contrasting ways
of old and new Clerkenwell — given fresh literary
fame in the *Riceyman Steps* of Arnold Bennett.
Eastward by London Wall, with fragments of the
ancient wall itself to be seen, and Bishopsgate, we
may go to another interesting old church and its surrounding in St. Helen's, not far from which stood for
many centuries the ancient Crosby Hall which was
some years since removed to Chelsea.   Whichever
way we go there are innumerable lesser by-ways
tempting to exploration and often revealing interesting survivals of the domestic architecture of the
past in carved doorways, decorative ironwork, fanlights and other details that remain though the
buildings to which they belong have become shops
or offices.   Sometimes, too, as between Fenchurch
Street and Eastcheap, we may happen upon old
houses up tiny courts that give yet fuller reminders

of the days when the citizens of London lived over or closely contiguous to their business premises.

IV

"To the left is the renowned realm of Alsatia, the Temple, the Mitre, and the abode of Richardson; to the right diverse abodes of Johnson; Chancery Lane, with Cowley's birthplace at the corner; Fetter Lane, where Dryden once lived; and Shire or Sheer Lane immortal for the Tatler."—*Leigh Hunt.*

"We are now in Fleet Street."—There has been much change not only in that famous highway but in its multitudinous by-ways since the genial essayist in his discursive saunter from St. Paul's to St. James's happened along here nearly ninety years ago. Then, there was no Ludgate Circus, and it was in the main a narrower Fleet Street wherein houses still remained representing the domestic architecture of the Tudors with its projecting upper storeys; and in the by-ways, downwards towards the Thames and upwards towards Holborn, changes have been not less sweeping. Traditions and associations remain to stir imagination and awaken sentiment, but of the actual things themselves that move us thus comparatively few remain, until we pass within the peaceful precincts of the Temple.

In a twisty by-way now strangely known as St. Bride's Avenue stands St. Bride's Church which, rebuilt by Wren after the Great Fire, is assuredly one of the most beautiful of the City's parish churches. It is interesting as the burial place of the cavalier lyrist Richard Lovelace, the sentimental printer-novelist Samuel Richardson, and the more famous printer Wynkyn de Worde. As Richardson lived long in the parish it may fairly be hazarded that he took the name of his roué in *Clarissa* from the poet buried in his parish church. In another of the by-ways here —Salisbury Square, then included in Salisbury Court —Richardson carried on his work as printer and as novelist, employing for a time as corrector of the press a greater novelist, Oliver Goldsmith. From the south-west corner of Salisbury Square, at the top of the strangely named Primrose Hill, is to be had the most beautiful view of the lovely tiered spire of St. Bride's. At No. 13 Salisbury Court is to be seen a plaque indicating the site of the house wherein the diarist Samuel Pepys was born — a site only lately identified.

The many streets, courts, and alleys that run river-wards from Fleet Street penetrated in olden times that Alsatia which was bordered by the muddy fore-shore of the Thames. Many of the twisty ways that remain hint at what a warren it must have been when the upper storeys of the houses almost met overhead. How Alsatia during the seventeenth century formed a sanctuary for all sorts and conditions of "wanted" persons who here sought refuge from the law is well shown in certain of the Restoration dramas — most notably in Shadwell's lively *The Squire of Alsatia*—and in certain chapters of Scott's *Fortunes of Nigel*. The district long retained privileges of sanctuary attached to the old monastery of the Carmelites, or White Friars, that stood hereabouts until dispossessed by Henry the Eighth. The district is still known as Whitefriars, and many place-names old and new recall the ancient foundation. Though the by-ways hereabouts have but little to hold the visitors' attention now, some of the lesser ones are worth visiting to "spring the imagination" concerning the past. Hanging Sword Alley, starting out of and then running closely parallel with Whitefriars Street, a narrow cañoned footway between the backs of high buildings, is perhaps the most notable of the Alsatian ways remaining, though projecting timbers appear to have given way in the eighteenth century to the sheer flatness of brick. Here, it may be recalled, Dickens placed the private lodgings of that extremely unpleasant person Mr. Jerry Cruncher.

Immediately west of Whitefriars lies the Temple's more or less enclosed network of by-ways wherein are to be found far more visible examples connected with a storied past that takes us far back in history and offers a wealth of such personal association as provides the most pervading charm to a locality. Here in the beautiful old Temple Church, with their effigies before us, we may recall the old Knights Templar who were organized early in the twelfth century with the knightly object of maintaining a right of way for pilgrims to the Holy Land; here are the gardens wherein leaders of the rival factions plucked those red and white blossoms which gave name to the consequent sanguinary Wars of the Roses of the fifteenth century; here we may visit the Halls of the Temple—that of the Middle Temple being a fine and interesting example of Tudor architecture; while at the top of Middle Temple Lane we have an engaging, scrap of the domestic architecture of the same period still surviving. Hereabouts we may in imagination walk with many later Templars of literature who have given new and gracious memories to the place: Johnson and Goldsmith, Lamb and Thackeray, and many more. Though in all too many instances the homes in which the men named sojourned have been replaced by newer buildings, their haunts retain much of that old-world charm which has made the Temple beloved of successive generations.

To the north of Fleet Street — between it and
Holborn—are by-ways scarcely less interesting. Here,
even within the memory of the middle-aged, the
hand of change has been more marked, though here
and there may be seen some noteworthy survivals.
In shabby Nevill's Court, running eastward from mid-
Fetter Lane, seventeenth- and eighteenth-century
houses yet remain, with tiny forecourt "gardens",
rare reminders of the time when this was still to a
considerable extent a residential district. Further
to the north, linking Fetter Lane and Bartlett's
Buildings, is Bartlett's Passage, near to which a
century or more ago was another alleyway wherein
was a day school in which Charles Lamb passed
some time before he proceeded to Christ's Hospital.
In Bartlett's Buildings and the neighbouring Thavies
Inn may still be seen some good carven doorways
and other reminders of days when the business
premises of the present were comfortable dwelling
houses.

Across Holborn from here are Ely Place and
Hatton Garden, both cut from the grounds of that
town mansion which Queen Elizabeth compelled the
Bishop of Ely to hand over to her supple favourite
Christopher Hatton. The "garden" which retains
the Lord Chancellor's name has become the Tom
Tiddler's ground of dealers in diamonds and other

THE RECORD OFFICE, FROM CLIFFORD'S INN

Extending from Chancery Lane to Fetter Lane, the handsome Record Office stands just to the
north of the old brick buildings of Clifford's Inn which are marked for early demolition.

precious stones. From Ely Place to Hatton Garden runs Mitre Court, within it an isolated old inn with a mitre let into the wall—a mitre which tradition likes to regard as a remnant of the old-time episcopal residence. In and about the neighbouring Saffron Hill are established many of London's Italian itinerant vendors of various wares.

Returning across Holborn to our Fleet Street district by way of Fetter Lane we find that linking by-way, though near the lower end dignified by the handsome Record Office, and with a story dating back over six hundred years, possesses yet little in itself to linger over. A little west of it stood Barnard's Inn, the hall of which is now the school of the Mercers' company—and west of that is the picturesque back-water of Staple Inn. Just off Fetter Lane, to the east in Fleur-de-Lis Court, is the dingy Newton Hall from which for a number of years Positivism was preached to congregations "fit but few". Dryden once dwelt in Fetter Lane, and the philosophical, having pondered the association with Positivism, may like to recall the fact that Hobbes lodged here at the time that his liberally abused *Leviathan* was published.

Most of the numerous by-ways tangled about the irregular tetragon bounded by Fleet Street and Holborn, Fetter Lane and Farringdon Street, have

been transmogrified within recent decades. Gone are
the old overhanging buildings that some of us re-
member in some of the courts, and most of the ways
now present a shabby mingling of quasi-old and un-
distinguished or frankly commonplace new. Wine
Office Court, but for its briefest beginning—between
the Olde Cheshire Cheese and oldish brick houses—
has become lamentably "improved" into a passage-
way of white-tiled buildings, and but for the old
hostelry can show little that met the eyes of Johnson
and Goldsmith. At the top this T-shaped court turns
right to Shoe Lane and left to Gough Square, wherein is perhaps the most interesting building within the
immediate area, interesting both as a good specimen
of the domestic architecture of the early eighteenth
century and for its personal association. This occupies
the western end of Gough Square, and is the house
wherein Samuel Johnson lived and worked for a
number of years. It is now preserved as a Johnsonian
Museum.

Many of the courts hereabouts retain the names
of old-time taverns, but few have any old-time
buildings remaining. In Crane Court, a cul-de-sac
terminated by the turreted red-brick building of the
Scottish Corporation, are still two or three handsome
old houses. Where the Scottish Corporation's building now stands stood the second home of the Royal

Society as they moved westward from Gresham
College in the City. Their one-time home in Crane
Court was burned down nearly fifty years ago.

V

"There Essex' stately pile adorn'd the shore,
    There Cecil's, Bedford's, Villiers'—now no more."
                                          —*John Gay*.

The poet's couplet indicates something of the way
in which the names of the by-ways neighbouring the
Strand are survivals from distant days when residences of the great nobles occupied much of the
ground between the City barrier of Temple Bar and
royal Westminster.   Here our by-ways, despite the
quaintness and antiquity of their names, have little
left of material ancientry to show, though Essex
Street with its plain old houses still terminates in a
flight of steps that once led down to the Thames
when that river was London's main highway, and that
now but leads us to the broad reclaimed tract of the
Embankment.   On the north side of the Strand
wholesale clearances of old network lanes and alleys
have been made, first for the Law Courts and later
for the making of Kingsway and Aldwych.   On the
south changes, apart from the Embankment, have
been less revolutionary, but have nevertheless been

sufficient to leave few of the by-ways with any
old-time characteristics.

Somerset House alone remains to remind us of the
days when the river-way was a way of noblemen's
mansions—and it does so but indirectly, for the range
of buildings as we know it was rebuilt between 1775-
1853. To the east of it runs Strand Lane, a footway
that appears to be a survival of an old public right of
way to the river between the grounds of two of the
great houses. In Strand Lane we may visit the ex-
cavated "Roman Bath", a link with the oldest historical
London. Apart from these, the old York Gate at the
foot of Buckingham Street and the Chapel Royal of
the Savoy, there is little to recall the splendid past
of this long riverside track, and the Savoy Church is
but the surviving fragment connected with the old
palace established here in the thirteenth century. As
burial place of Gavin Douglas, "the Chaucer of Scotland", it should be a place of pilgrimage for visitors
from the north.

Immediately to the west is a district the name of
which perpetuates in classic form the fact that it was
planned and built by brothers — the Adelphi. The
surname of this Scots quartet, Adam, and their
Christian names, John, Robert, James, and William,
are all commemorated in the dignified eighteenth-
century by-ways leading to Adelphi Terrace — that

DR. JOHNSON'S HOUSE

At the western end of Gough Square, this is one of the most interesting buildings
of the Fleet Street district. It was here that Samuel Johnson dwelt
while compiling his great *Dictionary*.

delightful row of houses which, overlooking the greenery of the Embankment and the river, has surely one of the most favoured situations in London. Here it is not surprising to find has been a favourite place of residence for many distinguished people from David Garrick to James Matthew Barrie. It is idle to protest against such change as is but the law of growth, yet it is permissible to hope that the threatened rebuilding of the Adelphi may be long postponed—that the small district may be left as a living specimen of eighteenth-century domestic architecture even as the row of Staple Inn buildings has been preserved in Holborn to indicate what Tudor London was like. The Adelphi is built over arches which were erected on the foreshore of the Thames to bring the buildings to the level of the Strand and above any danger of flooding from the river. Down the steps, that from the widened Strand have replaced the short steepness of Durham Street, may be seen the entrance to these Adelphi Arches. From John Street steeply merging into Duke Street we reach another series of name-linked by-ways—those representing in their full grouping George Villiers, Duke of Buckingham, even the preposition being employed to name Of Alley, now known as George Court, typical of the old-time alleys off the Strand. After another Villiers, it is said, is named that John Street which existed here twenty years before the names of the Adam brothers were given to the Adelphi ways. York Buildings was the general name for this group west of the Adelphi owing to the property having been in the possession of the Archbishop of York before passing into that of the Duke of Buckingham. The fine old watergate, though built by Inigo Jones for Buckingham, retains the name of York, and remains to remind us of the days when its base was lapped by the waters of the Thames.

Though but a narrow strip of buildings lies between the Strand and the river, it includes storied ways and some interesting survivals. The districts lying north of the Strand between it and the next east-and-west highway of Holborn and New Oxford Street are also rich in story and association, though modern changes, the clearing away of slum areas, the forming of new thoroughfares and the widening of old ones have within the past hundred years transformed almost the whole series of districts from vanished Shire Lane by Temple Bar to the engulfed Porridge Island where now is Trafalgar Square.

Covent Garden, with the by-ways leading to it, is so familiar to us as a crowded centre of flower, fruit, and vegetable marketing that it is not easy to realize that when the square was planned by Inigo Jones it was described as promising to be the finest in Europe, while the same architect's church at its western end was described as one of the most perfect pieces of architecture that the art of man could produce. Its old enclosed churchyard on the west is a delightful by-way. Now it is the market that has become the dominating feature, occupying the main part of the square and extending into numerous by-ways, and on market mornings, especially Saturdays in May and June, the sight here is one not to be forgotten, when all the floral wealth of spring seems to have been brought together for distribution over the great City.

In by-ways hereabouts may be recalled past events, past fashions, and past men of fame. In Maiden Lane was born our supreme master of the palette—J. M. W. Turner,—and in the same brief thoroughfare in earlier times dwelt Andrew Marvell and Voltaire. Bow Street was once the centre of West End fashion; at the westerly corner of Bow Street and Russell Street was the celebrated Wills' Coffee House where Dryden and Wycherley pontificated and Pope visited, and above which, a century later, Charles and Mary Lamb lived. Here we are roughly between—

"the houses twain
Of Covent Garden and of Drury Lane".

The whole district is crowded with interesting story and history though rebuilding is constantly changing its character.

Near to Drury Lane Theatre is a new theatre reviving the name of one that flourished in the time of Shakespeare, The Fortune, and in the neighbourhood there may be noticed a happy tendency to name the by-ways after people associated with the old-time "patent" theatres. Drury Lane itself, to the east, and St. Giles's to the north have been greatly changed within living memory and have little surviving left of the shabby picturesqueness of the past. Charing Cross Road, which to the west has been cut through from Trafalgar Square to Oxford Street, is neighboured by a number of modern theatres, and has in its midmost part come to be London's new Booksellers' Row. At its southern end the memorial to Edith Cavell stands between the church of St. Martin-in-the-Fields, and the National Portrait Gallery; near its northern end is the other church "in the fields", that of St. Giles.

VI

"I pray you, let us satisfy our eyes
With the memorials and the things of fame
That do renown this city."   —*Shakespeare.*

The by-ways of Westminster for the majority of us mean rather the ways about the neighbourhood of the Abbey than those of that City of Westminster which

QUEEN ANNE'S GATE, WESTMINSTER

The handsome red-brick mansions that remain a little to the south-west of
St. James's Park form one of the most pleasing survivals in domestic
architecture of that period the name of which they bear.

covers a considerable part of Central London, extending from Victoria in one direction to the Temple,
in another to Knightsbridge, and from the Thames
to the Marble Arch, Oxford Street, and Holborn.

Though to a great extent they have been rebuilt within the past half-century the by-ways in the
neighbourhood of Westminster Abbey are of the most
varied character, ranging from mean streets to mean
streets rebuilt into new importance; with, between
these as it were, and more attractive than either,
such streets of simple dignity with a gravely old-
fashioned aspect as Cowley Street, which with the
neighbouring Barton Street, is said to have been
built early in the eighteenth century by the actor
Barton Booth. The quaint, old, irregular houses
with panelled rooms that some of us knew in Great
College Street have given place to more pretentious
modern buildings; that one-sided street has become
renewed but still fronts the ancient wall enclosing
the Abbey precincts. At the western end of the
street a gateway gives on to the quiet quadrangle of
Dean's Yard, long the playground of the Westminster School boys, who later secured a more extensive ground in Vincent Square, part of the old-time
Tothill Fields, somewhat to the south-west.

Just south of Dean's Yard runs Tufton Street,
wherein will be observed the interesting, but archi-

tecturally insignificant, Royal Architectural Museum.

Up to within half a century ago there were still to be found in the by-ways of Westminster ancient houses with upper storeys overhanging the streets—now it is mainly in place-names that we get hints of ancientry so recently manifest. Broad and Little Sanctuary tell of old days when safety was to be sought within the precincts of great ecclesiastical foundations. Petty France—an ancient name happily restored — denotes where of old a French colony lived. Now it is mainly large buildings, blocks of offices, "mansions" of flats that are found in many of the Westminster by-ways lying to the west of the Abbey. Where Victoria Street was cut westward in the middle of last century was a veritable network of by-ways. Even where the by-ways have remained less drastically changed, south-westward of the Abbey there is little enough to recall the past. Winding and twisting ways will take us through a densely populated area to Pimlico and Vauxhall, more or less parallel with the riverside highway, past the back of the Tate Gallery and the site of the old Millbank Prison, beyond the Horseferry Road. Here at least we have name reminders of the past when, where Lambeth Bridge now is, was an old ferry for taking horses across the Thames, and here, on the Middlesex side, stood a mill. Romney Street, near by—which owes

its name to a peer, not to the painter—was of old
Vine Street, and is said traditionally to mark the
site of the vineyard at one time attached to the
royal palace of Westminster. In that "fam'd Vine
Street" it was that the eighteenth-century satirist
Charles Churchill was born, and he has given
it something of a bathetic fame in referring to it as
the place—

"Where Heav'n, the utmost wish of man to grant,
   Gave me an old House, and an older Aunt".

Just north of Romney Street is Smith Square,
long notable for its old houses and its singular
church of St. John the Evangelist, built in the early
part of the eighteenth century. This square and
Great Smith Street, somewhat to the north west of
it, received their names, as did so many of the
thoroughfares of the metropolis, from the ground
landlord in possession at the time when they were
laid out. In Great Smith Street — the prefatory
adjective of which is only suitable by comparison
with its neighbouring Little Smith Street — is the
main entrance of the Church House, designed as a
Parliament House for the Church of England. The
by-ways west of this street formed at one time the
"rookery" of Westminster, a low neighbourhood that
had grown up within the sanctuarial precincts of the

Abbey, but the improvement scheme of last century
swept it away. On the farther side of Victoria Street
the changes have been not less marked, perhaps
even more so, and though we may find names re-
miniscent of old Westminster association — Petty
France, Tothill Street, Caxton Street, and so on—
there is little to claim more than passing attention
in the ways between the omnibus highway of Victoria
Street and St. James's Park, though some handsome red-brick mansions about Queen Anne's Gate
still afford a pleasing picture. Passing by one of the
narrow ways into the park we may follow by-ways
through this green pleasaunce, with the massy Govern-
ment offices of Whitehall on the right and the
spacious extent of Buckingham Palace on the left
and so reach the by-ways that lie between the park
and Piccadilly, the heart of clubland. Here, along
part of the northern side of St. James's Park, is
Carlton House Terrace, interrupted by the Duke of
York's Column—and a little beyond it is Pall Mall,
two of the most world-famous amongst London's
by-ways. The former is the most notable, as it is
the most central, residential terrace for prominent
and wealthy persons, though it has lately been invaded from clubland. Pall Mall has for generations
been celebrated as one of the chief social centres of
London. Writing of it over half a century ago

Thackeray summed up its character and associations in a remarkable passage.

" Pall Mall is the great social Exchange of London now — the mart of news, of politics, of scandal, of rumour—the English town, so to speak, where men discuss the last dispatch from the Crimea, the last speech of Lord Derby, the next move of Lord John. And, now and then, to a few anti-quarians, whose thoughts are with the past rather than the present, it is a memorial of old times and old people, and Pall Mall is our Palmyra. Look! About this spot Tom of Ten Thousand was killed by Königsmarck's gang. In that great red house Gainsborough lived, and Culloden Cumberland, George III's uncle. Yonder is Sarah Marlborough's palace, just as it stood when that termagant occupied it. At 25 Walter Scott used to live; at the house, now No. 79, and occupied by the Society for the Propagation of the Gospel in Foreign Parts, resided Mrs. Eleanor Gwynn, comedian. How often has Queen Caroline's chair issued from under yonder arch! All the men of the Georges have passed up and down the street. It has seen Walpole's chariot, and Chatham's sedan; and Fox, Gibbon, Sheridan, on their way to Brookes's; and stately William Pitt stalking on the arm of Dundas; and Hanger and Tom Sheridan reeling out of Raggett's; and Byron

limping into Wattier's; and Swift striding out of
Bury Street; and Mr. Addison and Dick Steele, both
perhaps a little the better for liquor; and the Prince
of Wales, and the Duke of York clattering over the
pavement; and Johnson, counting the posts along
the streets, after dawdling before Dodsley's window;
and Harry Walpole hobbling into his carriage, with
a gimcrack just bought out at Christie's; and
George Selwyn sauntering into White's."

From the matter of this somewhat lengthy quota-
tion it may be recognized that much the same
kaleidoscopic history might be presented of any
part of London, for the London enthusiast who
described the Thames as "liquid history" might have
gone much further and described every one of these
old thoroughfares as compact of the very stuff of history itself. Sedan chairs and chariots were duly
followed by carriages, and motor-cars have now
taken their place, but still by-ways such as Pall
Mall maintain much of their traditional character.
Just to the north, between it and Jermyn Street, is
St. James's Square—residence of many great folks
from Pitt to Gladstone, and every side street here
has its association for those who would praise famous
men. Here we are in the heart of St. James's, in
all the by-ways of which are to be recalled memories
of men and events: the pleasant stately houses that

form the linking ways westward to Arlington Street and the Green Park have for a couple of centuries been associated with rank and fashion, though in changing conditions many of them are being converted to purposes other than residential.

VII

"I like to walk among the Hebrews of Wardour Street, and fancy the place, as it once was, crowded with chairs and gilt chariots, and torches flashing in the hands of running footmen. I have a grim pleasure in thinking that Golden Square was once the resort of the aristocracy, and Monmouth Street the delight of the genteel world."

—*Thackeray.*

Bounded roughly by Oxford Street, Regent Street, and Shaftesbury Avenue, though extending beyond the last-named highway of theatres, the large roughly triangular district generally known as Soho has come to be famed chiefly as a "colony" of foreigners resident in London, as a centre of old curiosity shops, and also as a centre of popular and quasi-fashionable "Bohemian" restaurants; indeed, the last-named may be said to afford the dominating note to-day. In many of the narrow ways here we may find old house fronts, ornamental door-knockers, and fanlights dating back to the days of sedan chairs and link-boys, survivals from the days when, at the close of the

seventeenth century, this district came to be developed
for residential purposes, and for some time enjoyed
the reputation of being a fashionable locality until
still farther westward the tide of Fashion took its
way.

Apart from such survivals of the domestic architecture of our forbears, there is not very much to take
the eye of the wanderer in the by-ways hereabouts,
though the whole district is redolent of memories.
The church of St. Anne, Soho—where the modern
highway of Shaftesbury Avenue cuts across the old
by-way of Wardour Street,—is notable to lovers of
literature as the burial-place of William Hazlitt, the
essayist, whose later years were passed in furnished
lodgings in the neighbouring Frith Street where,
in the presence of Charles Lamb, he passed away
with the words, "Well, I've had a happy life". King
Theodore of Corsica, also buried at St. Anne's, probably compels but few pilgrims thither.

That the whole of Soho district, centring in Soho
Square—or King's Square as it was originally
named—was for some time a fashionable residential
district, is made plain to the observant wanderer
about its tangled ways. It has, however, come to be
dominated by commerce and manufactures, and from
occasional turnings lofty chimney stacks may be seen.
Among the surrounding streets are some particularly

SHEPHERD'S MARKET, MAYFAIR

Entrance to a scrap of eighteenth-century London that remains between Piccadilly
and Curzon Street. The market owes its name not to any pastoral
association but to a one-time owner of the property.

favoured by the trades associated with music, and
many shops of dealers in delicatessen, newspapers and
books, and other things imported from abroad such
as might be looked for in one of the chief centres in
which sojourners from the Continent are accustomed
to congregate.

Great emporiums form one boundary of the district
front on Regent Street, while several theatres are
along the Shaftesbury Avenue side. In the network of small streets, courts, and alleys are to be
found many curious by-ways of London life, queer little
restaurants patronized by special circles of customers,
other restaurants that have come to be the recognized
rendezvous for fashionable Bohemianism, and small
clubs associated with the nationals of the various
foreign colonies resident in London, and quaintly
named clubs housed in the picturesquely adapted
stables of one-time mews fallen into disuse through
the all-pervading triumph of petrol. It is indeed a
district of striking contrasts, for we may pass almost
directly from the broad highway of the renewed Regent
Street, with the fresh stone façades of its great shops,
to narrow ways and a colourful street market—even
to a mere flagged passage where the shops so nearly
meet across the way that we have something of a
reminder of the times when such alleys were common
features of city life. This narrow way, Walker's Court,

connects Little Pulteney Street with Peter Street and
Berwick Street, all of which together form one of the
most notable of London's colourful street markets—
little known to thousands of those who pass within
a few yards of it at Piccadilly Circus or along Shaftesbury Avenue.

Though two or three streets cross, or nearly cross,
the Soho area—as for example Wardour Street, which
has adjectivally come to signify the sham antique—it is
mostly a criss-cross of shorter ways with two notable
squares—that which gives its name to the whole
district in the angle formed by Oxford Street and
Charing Cross Road, and to the south-west that Golden
Square, which, as Charles Dickens tells us, had
already come down in the world and was largely
given over to lodgers in the days when Mr. Ralph
Nickleby dwelt in one of its houses and Mr. Newman
Noggs lodged with the Kenwigs family in a shabby
street near by. Still can it be said that the square
"is not exactly in anybody's way to or from any-
where". Though "has been" is written in many of
the ways of Soho, the wave of commercial rebuilding
is considerably changing its borders, and near its
north-western corner the range of neo-Tudor premises
calls for particular mention.

VIII

"Give me the sweet shady side of Pall Mall."
—*Charles Morris.*

From the days when noblemen's mansions bordered
the Thames from the city boundaries to the neighbourhood of the Royal Palace of Westminster, there has
been a constant succession of districts to which the
well-to-do have moved, pressed more or less westward
by the ever-growing commercial community. Covent
Garden and Bloomsbury, St. James's, Mayfair, and
Belgravia, have all at one time or another been looked
upon as centres wherein the socially successful were
housed. Mayfair, which is one of the latest and most
notable of them, seems to be gradually penetrated by
shopping streets, and will seemingly follow the usual
course of decline and fall—will perhaps prove the last
of London's special Society areas, for development of
the motor car has so shortened distances that well-
to-do folks can dwell farther afield and still remain
within easy access of the social amenities of the
metropolis, while the growth of the habit of utilizing
hotels for residential purposes is tending to the same
end.

The area of Mayfair may be regarded as that rough
parallelogram bounded on the west by Hyde Park,

on the east by Bond Street, and north and south respectively by Oxford Street and Piccadilly. Within it we find the green oases of Grosvenor and Berkeley Squares, and numerous by-ways the names of which are familiar as those wherein Rank and Fashion have long been at home. Near Devonshire House—over which hangs the shadow of impending change—was at one time held in the month of May that annual fair which has given its name to the district; and a little to the west of it (between Piccadilly and Curzon Street) is yet to be seen that Shepherd's Market— the name is landlordly, not pastoral—which is a surviving scrap of eighteenth-century London lingering amid changed surroundings. Under an archway, from Shepherd's Market we pass into fashionable Curzon Street, in which, at No. 19, the Earl of Beaconsfield died. To the left we may pass to a ramifying series of streets in the heart of Mayfair, or to the right, by Bolton Row, reach the narrow passage—presumably an ancient footpath preserved from the distant days when there were fields hereabouts—that bisects the extensive gardens between Devonshire House and Berkeley Square.

Through all the manifold by-ways of Mayfair we find small houses or large mansions mostly wearing the aspect of comfortable wealth, with here and there narrow mews wherein, before the coming of the motor-

LANCASTER GATE FOUNTAIN, KENSINGTON GARDENS

One of the many beauty spots of the linked Kensington Gardens and Hyde Park; it is close to the Bayswater Road, yet unknown to many who pass along that broad highway.

car, were housed the carriages and horses of the well-
to-do. Here and there are interesting old ironwork
and even surviving examples of the iron extinguishers
at which the link boys of the past put out their torches.

If we cross the broad highway of Oxford Street
we pass into what may be regarded as a northerly
extension of Mayfair, though the name of that district
does not appear properly to extend to it. Here are
Portman, Bryanston, and Manchester Squares, which,
with their linking by-ways, have been associated with
wealthy residents. It is this district—with its western
"expatiation" along the north side of Hyde Park, to
which the social satirists of some years ago gave the
name of "Tyburnia", from the sinister "Tyburn tree"
or gallows that of old stood somewhat to the west of
the Marble Arch. The squares and by-ways here are
formed of solidly comfortable houses, with but little
to call for a lingering stay. An exception must be
made in the case of Manchester Square, the north side
of which is occupied by one of the most notable of
our treasure-houses of art. This is Hertford House,
in which is to be seen the great Wallace Collection of
fine pictures, armour, furniture, &c. A little to the east
of it runs the narrow tortuosity of Marylebone Lane,
which later becomes the High Street. The last
house in this latter thoroughfare, in the direction of
the Marylebone Road, was for some time the home

of Charles Dickens, then at the height of his fame.

An extension of Mayfair lies eastward of Bond Street and reaches to Regent Street—a district which, while it has been largely annexed by commercialism, includes in Hanover Square a centre famous in social chronicles, for a little off the square, in George Street, is St. George's Church, which has long been regarded as the appropriate scene of Society weddings. From the end of Savile Row—traditionally the oracular near centre of fashionable tailordom — runs the quaint by-way of the Albany, a short covered way on either side of which is a row of "maisonnettes", which was built in the early years of last century to serve as bachelor chambers, inhabited by a succession of famous residents from Byron to Macaulay and Gladstone, and figures frequently in fiction as the home of gilded youth.

IX

"Oh, mine in snows and summer heats,
These good old Tory brick-built streets!
My eye is pleased with all it meets
In Bloomsbury."

Bloomsbury is a district in the by-ways of which we shall find the British Museum, the Foundling Hospital, and University College, with literary and personal associations of endless variety. The district, for our present purposes, may be said to extend from Tottenham Court Road on the west to Gray's Inn Road on the east, and from Euston Road on the north to New Oxford Street and High Holborn on the south—something not far short of a square mile in area, its innumerable ways inviting to recollections of all manner of famous men and women: Thackeray lived here in his early married life (13 Great Coram Street); and Dickens at the house in Doughty Street (No. 48) which remains much as it was when the story of Pickwick and his companions was being written there, and also at Tavistock House at the corner of the square of the same name. John Ruskin was born at 54 Hunter Street, while those men of fame who have sojourned in Bloomsbury by-ways would afford a catalogue of many of the most famous names in nineteenth-century literature and art. Among those who dwelt in the district for shorter or longer periods were Shelley (26 Marchmont Street); Carlyle (6 Woburn Buildings and 5 Ampton Street); Darwin (110 Gower Street); John Leech (32 Brunswick Square); Christina Rossetti (5 Endsleigh Gardens and 30 Torrington Square); while Dante Gabriel Rossetti, William Morris, Burne-Jones, and Ford Madox Brown are all associated with 17 Red Lion Square—and some of them with other Bloomsbury houses also.

From that dingy square came much of the joyous note of the Pre-Raphaelite Brotherhood, and the beginnings of Morris's renaissance of domestic decoration. Bloomsbury had already its association with art in Sass's Academy (6 Charlotte Street, the southern continuation of Gower Street), the first school of the kind established in London, and one that counted among its pupils Millais, Frith, and Edward Lear, whose literary "nonsense" has eclipsed his pictorial landscapes.

Owing to its central position—and perhaps also to its lying immediately to the south of the great London railway termini of Euston, St. Pancras, and King's Cross, Bloomsbury has come to be regarded as a neighbourhood wholly given over to lodgings, boarding-houses and hotels. Such have not, however, yet monopolized the whole of Bloomsbury; still do its comfortable streets and squares afford private homes for many people, though some of those streets and squares have during recent years been in course of change: Southampton Row and Great Russell Street, Russell Square and the tract immediately behind the British Museum, for instance, have greatly changed within the memory of many of us.

The clearance behind the British Museum is a reminder that a century and a half ago open fields stretched thence to Paddington and Primrose Hill, and that in the near neighbourhood of the Museum was the mysterious Field of the Forty Footsteps, or the Brothers' Steps. The story ran that at the time of the Monmouth Rebellion two brothers there fought a duel in which both were slain, and the footmarks made during their terrible encounter, as well as the places where their bodies lay, remained ever afterwards bare of any herbage. Sinister as this story is, however, it has been powerless to keep the fatal field free of bricks and mortar.

Of the British Museum itself little can here be said beyond the fact that it may well be regarded as the supreme sight to be found in the by-ways of Bloomsbury. Within it is the world's greatest library of books, and the greatest collection of miscellaneous "specimens" from all lands and all ages, that may be said to illustrate with actuality the whole range of man's knowledge recorded in the millions of volumes.

Another building that calls for special mention is the Foundling Hospital in Guilford Street — a place erected a few years before Montague House became the British Museum. Standing well back from the road, and flanked east and west by Mecklenburg and Brunswick Squares, the Foundling occupies one of the most open sites left in Central London. Captain Coram's great institution is, however, after nearly two centuries of existence, to be moved to country surroundings and its grounds will presumably be built over. The Hospital with its many small inhabitants is one of the most moving of places to be visited, and the Sunday service at the chapel something not to be forgotten, as William Blake wrote:

"Oh, what a multitude they seemed, these flowers of London town!
Seated in companies they sit, with radiance all their own;
The hum of multitudes was there, but multitudes of lambs,
Hundreds of little boys and girls raising their innocent hands."

To the south-eastward Bloomsbury touches the confines of Gray's Inn with its pleasant greenery of trees and turf, its old hall, solidly comfortable looking chambers, and recollections of Lord Verulam and other dignitaries of law and literature. The neighbourhood of the Inn is much inhabited by lawyers, the broad way of pleasant old-fashioned residences, Bedford Row, still symbolizing as it were all lawyerdom. Behind its eastern side runs the narrow Jockey Field Row, the name of which seems to suggest a somewhat distant past when the gentlemen of Gray's Inn were able to indulge in equestrian exercise in fields contiguous to their Inn.

Eastward from Bloomsbury, towards Clerkenwell and the City, are many and varied by-ways, inviting

LANCELOT PLACE, KNIGHTSBRIDGE

A quaint bit of a one-time village long since absorbed by London's growth that may be seen
within but a few yards of one of London's largest departmental stores.

now to lingeringly residential places in some of the
squares that lie about the slope that leads up to
Islington, and now to Leather Lane and Saffron Hill,
and so to Hatton Garden, and beyond to the Charterhouse, and a variety of other places glanced at in
earlier pages.

X

"Its manor house, its college, its botanic garden, its
amusements at Ranelagh, its waterworks, its buns, its
china and its custard."—*Peter Cunningham.*

Not by any means exhaustive was this list of things
for which the one-time village of Chelsea—now a
populous riverside district—has from time to time been
famous. Its most recent fame has perhaps been won
by the notable folks who have made their homes in
its olden ways, and by the fact of its being a centre
specially favoured by artists. There is much to be
seen—and far more to be recalled—in the by-ways
that turn inland from the river front, stretching from
Chelsea Bridge to the gasworks, and the other by-ways
that link them. And, firstly, perhaps mention should
be made of Crosby Hall, that old transplanted building
which is to be seen near the corner where Danvers
Street turns off from famed Cheyne Walk just eastward of Battersea Bridge. Though new walls had to be

made, the doorways, windows, roof, and other details
are those of the fifteenth-century building that stood
until a few years ago in Bishopsgate in the City.
Though amid new surroundings, Crosby Hall affords
an unequalled example of the home of a wealthy
citizen of London of some four hundred years ago.

Chelsea's associations with men of fame in literature
and the arts may be said to vie with those of Bloomsbury in number. Apart from those who made their
homes along Cheyne Walk—Turner, Whistler, Rossetti, and many more—are others who dwelt in the
quiet turnings. Principal shrine of the district for
many visitors is that modest house on the east side of
Cheyne Row where Thomas Carlyle lived and worked
for many years. Preserved as it is as a Carlyle
Museum, we may therein see much that was there
when it was the home of the "Sage of Chelsea". No
longer do the windows of Carlyle's house look out on
hayfields, as they did when he first went there. Yet
still much of the description which he gave of Chelsea
as a whole may be said to be applicable. "Chelsea
is a singular heterogeneous kind of spot, very dirty
and confused in some places, quite beautiful in others,
abounding in antiquities and the traces of great men—
Sir Thomas More, Steele, Smollett, &c. Our Row,
which for the last three doors or so is a street, and
none of the noblest, runs out upon a 'Parade' (perhaps

they call it), running along the shore of the river, a broad highway with huge shady trees, boats lying moored, and a smell of shipping and tar." The Parade is that Cheyne Walk from which Turner and Whistler made immortal pictures and which has come to be marked among its huge trees with the statue of one of Chelsea's "great men"—Thomas Carlyle himself.

Farther up Cheyne Row, where it narrows towards the busy highway of the King's Road, lived Leigh Hunt. A little beyond again, in the easterly Glebe Place, the remains of an old Tudor building—traditionally known as King Henry VIII's Hunting Lodge—have been tastefully incorporated into an artist-home with a stone-flagged garden in which is still demonstrated Chelsea's traditional floral fertility. Here and elsewhere in the district are blocks of "studios" arranged for the convenience of many artists drawn to a district that has become, as it were, especially consecrated to Art. Still may we mark that heterogeneity which struck Carlyle close upon a hundred years ago, passing from narrow ways of low-built houses with small forecourt gardens to the blare of the town in the highways that go on westward to Brompton, Fulham, and Hammersmith, with their numerous byways of associations into which we cannot here pass.

Northwards across those highways we find how near is Kensington to Chelsea—or at least the southern

extension of that quadripartite Kensington to which
the one-time village has given its name. Perhaps the
most appropriate point from which to start a brief
review of Kensington by-ways is from that Palace, "of
homely fireside character", which stands to the west
of those Gardens which a modern magician has newly
peopled for us with Peter Pan, the immortally young,
and the fairies. Kensington Palace, a red brick building with royal memories from the time of William III,
has much to show the visitor, but in this cursory
ramble through by-ways, we can do little more than
mention it. The hastiest visit, however, especially if
it be paid in spring or summer, should include a pause
at the delightful Sunk Garden, a green and flowery
parterre unknown to many Londoners who are familiar
with a somewhat similar quadrangle of formal garden-
ing at Hampton Court. In front of the Palace extend
Kensington Gardens and Hyde Park, where spring
most beautifully comes to London, and many by-ways
invite us among fine trees, through shrubberies, or
along the Long Water and Serpentine. Where the
West Bourne comes into the Gardens at the fountain
near Lancaster Gate, and where it leaves the Park
by Knightsbridge, are particularly beautiful spots.
Near to the former stands Frampton's fascinating
statue of Peter Pan, whom Barrie has created as
presiding genius of the place.

West of the Palace—between the two main western highways—runs Kensington Palace Gardens, the substantial houses of which include (No. 2) that built by William Makepeace Thackeray for himself, and wherein he died. Immediately west, again, comes the criss-crossing of by-ways about Campden Hill—with memories of Macaulay, John Leech, and other celebrities—on the farther side of which is the beautiful expanse of Holland Park, famous as a centre of London's social and intellectual life as long ago as when Joseph Addison lived there a couple of hundred years back. Between the park that bears one of the titles of Addison's countess-wife and the road to which his name has been given are some handsome houses built by artists and others in the latter half of last century. Principal of these, from the sightseer's point of view, is Leighton House in Holland Park Road—the sumptuous home of that master painter of the sumptuous, Lord Leighton, P.R.A., preserved by way of memorial much as it was in his time.

Crossing the main highway about this point to the southward we may reach the Earl's Court district by way of Edwardes Square, the large central garden and low-built houses of which impart a pleasant air of spaciousness. Many are the literary associations here around. Leigh Hunt lived for some years in the Square itself, while in the highway terrace that backs

on to its north side, at different periods lived Elizabeth
Inchbald and Walter Pater—as striking a contrast as
literature, with all its variety, could well show. Many
by-ways of pleasant comfortable houses, with occasional
terraces, low-built and with a little garden to each
house, are reminders of days not so long ago
when this was a new residential district. Now it is
a rapidly changing one: modest villa homes giving
place to pretentious "mansions", and some of the
streets of substantial houses being invaded by shops
and business premises. Southward by-ways will take
us into Chelsea, and eastward ones to Knightsbridge
and Belgravia—leading in either direction to many
of those pleasant oases of greenery, the residential
"squares" which formed a special feature in the
laying out of new building areas in the eighteenth
and nineteenth centuries. Here and there too we may
light upon picturesque nooks and corners overlooked
by those who keep to the highways, as in the narrow-
ing angle where the main Knightsbridge and Brompton Roads near their junction; there in Lancelot
Place is a group of small cottages that might well
be a relic of the one-time village of Knightsbridge, strangely contrasting with the modernities
of barracks, hotels, and super-shops.

XI

"In the south suburbs, at the Elephant."
                                        —Shakespeare.

Although the hostelry of which Shakespeare made
mention lay in the south suburbs of that vague city
in Illyria in which the scenes of *Twelfth Night*
are placed, the line is peculiarly applicable to London,
inasmuch as a meeting-point of many highways
about a mile southward of the most northerly bend
of London's river is popularly known as "the
Elephant". The highways which lead thence upwards to the various bridges and downwards through
suburbs extending away into Surrey and Kent, are
linked by by-ways innumerable, which in a necessarily
cursory survey must be left unexplored. Here we
limit ourselves more or less to some of those by-
ways which neighbour the right bank of the river—
for these pass through the most storied parts of the
south side—though it may be hinted that excursions
radially extended from "the Elephant" would take us
to Clapham, Camberwell, Dulwich, the Norwoods,
Blackheath, Bermondsey, and other one-time villages
become urbanized, each the centre of much historical
or personal association.

If we cross London Bridge we are at once in

what is now a busy railway and commercial centre, and also probably in what is the oldest part of transpontine London. Here we are at once in Southwark and though we find the by-ways hereabouts are now largely given up to factories, warehouses, and other business premises, there is much within easy reach of the southern end of London Bridge to stir the imagination. Eastward, if we follow as closely as may be the course of the river, we get glimpses from dockside turnings of the busiest parts of the great waterway, with views across the crowded "Pool" to the Custom House and the long-famed Tower, and then after passing the lofty Tower Bridge—approached on this side from strangely named Pickle-herring Street—our riverside glimpses give us views of dockside warehouses, dock entrances, and quaint old bits of waterside London. Following along here we come to Bermondsey, Rotherhithe, and Deptford, all of them associated with England's long sea-story— with, facing us on the farther bank beyond the shipping (ever shifting yet ever seemingly the same) other places linked with the past and present of our seafaring population, Wapping, Shadwell, and Limehouse.

Immediately to the west of London Bridge rises the tower of that cathedral church of St. Saviour's— once know as St. Mary Overie — which is one of the

OLD BARRACK YARD, BELGRAVIA

Representative of many old bits to be found in nooks and corners of the great city, Old Barrack
Yard is "within a stone's throw" of Buckingham Palace grounds and Hyde Park Corner.

principal shrines for literary pilgrims to Southwark, and one calling for a lingering visit. A little beyond the church and we reach Bankside, now broken by the southern approach to Southwark Bridge but still affording notable cross-river views of the City of London. From this view-point, too, one receives a definite impression of the fact that the cathedral of St. Paul's is builded upon a hill.

Though Southwark Street has been cut through to form a link with the highway approaches to London and Blackfriars Bridges, and though the streets old and new that turn and twist about the neighbourhood are largely made up of factories, printing and other works, yet the riverside part especially is attractive for the views it affords and for the memories it evokes. Hereabouts stood that old Globe Theatre which looms large in the story of Shakespeare and Elizabethan drama — its site long since occupied by a brewery which in the eighteenth century comes into the story of Samuel Johnson; while hereabouts also were the Bear Garden and the Paris Garden at which Tudor Londoners took their pleasures roughly at bear-baitings and such-like crude forms of entertainment.

Somewhat to the south where Great Dover Street and other thoroughfares branch from the Borough High Street may be explored the neighbourhood of the old Marshalsea Prison — already described as "mean and ruinous" in the mid-part of the eighteenth century—made famous by the story of *Little Dorrit*. Far older, however, are the literary associations of Southwark, beginning as they do with the very beginning of our modern literature:

> "On a day
> In Southwark at the Tabard as I lay,
> Ready to wenden on my pilgrimage
> To Canterbury with full devout courage,
> At night were come into that hostelry
> Well nine-and-twenty in a company,
> Of sundry folk, by adventure y-falle
> In fellowship, and pilgrims were they all,
> That toward Canterbury woulden ride."

Where Chaucer's hostelry stood still stands a Tabard Inn—to quicken the memory, however, by name and site alone, for the ancient inn was destroyed half a century ago. We may, however, still see in the "George" here what is perhaps London's best remaining example of the old-time open-yarded inns, though this after being destroyed by fire was rebuilt in Stuart days.

Passing through by-ways that neighbour the Borough High Street and Road we may come to a junction of highways at St. George's Circus—a parting of the ways whence by radiating roads we may reach over half a dozen of the bridges across the Thames:

Lambeth, Westminster, Charing Cross, Waterloo, Blackfriars, Southwark, and London.   Here we are but a little northwards of that other radial centre already mentioned, "the Elephant".   The Lambeth Road trending to the southwestward in little more than half a mile reaches Lambeth Bridge—that spot which in antiquarian interest most nearly approximates to our starting-place at London Bridge.   Here was the old horse-ferry across the Thames—seemingly the only point at which, for centuries, horses were habitually taken over other than by the old London Bridge — so that we are here rather on a highway than on a by-way.   Looking up-stream, before leaving the bridge-end, we have on our left the Albert Embankment leading to Vauxhall — famed for old-time gaiety—and Kennington Oval where cricketers do constant homage to "Willow the King".   On the opposite side of the river, a prominent feature is the handsome Tate Gallery of British Art.   Looking down-stream we have the beautiful range of the Houses of Parliament, its fretted river front between the fine Victoria Tower and the loftier Clock Tower, affording a striking contrast with the red brick of the St. Thomas's Hospital range on the right.   Close to us are the ancient walls and dingy red brick of Lambeth Palace, for centuries the London residence of successive Archbishops of Canterbury, and in parts one

of the oldest of London's buildings. The gate-house
dates from the fifteenth century, while the chapel is
some two hundred years older still.

By the terrace walk along the riverside front of
the hospital, with one of the grandest of the many
fine and varied views that the south side affords, we
soon reach Westminster Bridge and that strikingly
handsome London County Hall which is giving new
dignity to this bank of the Thames, and opening
visions of a time when the whole shall be worthy of
the great City. If we follow the by-ways that keep
closest to the river, from brief turnings that here and
again reach to the wharf side we may get fresh and
striking views across the river to the roofs and
towers above the trees of the avenued Embankment
and its gardens, with now the memorial to British
airmen who fell in the Great War — a modern and
moving version of the Winged Victory—and now the
ancient Egyptian monolith ("Cleopatra's Needle")
breaking the line of the riverside balustrade. The
Charing Cross railway bridge forms, it is true, an
unsightly feature, but hope tells a flattering tale of
its possible replacement by something worthier of the
position. Up-stream and down-stream are Westminster
and Waterloo Bridges in dignified contrast with the
impudent iron contraption in between.

For maybe the vast majority of Londoners and

sightseeing visitors the views of London's Thames are those of the south side seen from the Embankment—views as some of us think made hideous by modern manifestations of advertising; far finer, far worthier of the great City are the views to be had in the reverse direction, from bridge-ends or by-ways along the southern side.